BASE JUMPING

Base jumpers jump from structures such as cliffs.

BASE JUMPING

ODYSSEYS

ERIC RAYMOND SAVON

CREATIVE EDUCATION · CREATIVE PAPERBACKS

Published by Creative Education and Creative Paperbacks
P.O. Box 227, Mankato, Minnesota 56002
Creative Education and Creative Paperbacks are imprints of
The Creative Company
www.thecreativecompany.us

Design by Graham Morgan
Art direction by Tom Morgan
Edited by Kremena Spengler

Images by Alamy Stock Photo/ABACAPRESS, 66, blickwinkel/Royer, cover;
Getty Images/Andia, 8, 24, Eye Ubiquitous, 48, Fred Marie/Art in All of Us, 37,
62, MAXIM MARMUR, 61, Mickey Pfleger, 70-71, Mohd Samsul Mohd Said, 11,
VCG, 32-33, VW Pics, 69; Unsplash/Jonathan Francis, 46, Kamil
Pietrzak, 50, Lane Smith, 29; Wikimedia Commons/Antonio
Carnicero, 22, Grunertrond, 26, Ka23 13, 58, Kontizas Dimitrios, 6,
42, Leo-setä, 54, SMU Libraries Digital Collections, 12, Soldatini
Alberto Mario (progettista)/Somenzi Vittorio (progettista),
18, U.S. Air Force/Volkmar Wentzel, 75, United States Air Force, 4-5, Fausto
Veranzio, 17, Xof711, 2

Library of Congress Cataloging-in-Publication Data
Names: Savon, Eric Raymond, author. Title: Base jumping / By Eric Raymond
Savon.
Description: Mankato, Minnesota : Creative Education and Creative Paperbacks,
    [2025] | Series: Odysseys in extreme sports | Includes bibliographical
    references and index. | Audience: Ages 12-15 | Audience: Grades 7-9 |
    Summary: "Get a rush with this title for high school readers about
    BASE jumping, the extreme sport of leaping off fixed objects with a
    parachute. Includes skills and equipment needed, a glossary, index,
    and further resources"– Provided by publisher.
Identifiers: LCCN 2024030289 (print) | LCCN 2024030290 (ebook) | ISBN
    9798889893080 (library binding) | ISBN 9781682776742 (paperback) | ISBN
    9798889894193 (ebook)
Subjects: LCSH: BASE jumping–Juvenile literature.
Classification: LCC GV770.26 .R64 2025 (print) | LCC GV770.26 (ebook) | DDC
    796.04/6–dc23/eng/20240702
LC record available at https://lccn.loc.gov/2024030289
LC ebook record available at https://lccn.loc.gov/2024030290

Printed in China

BASE jumping from a balloon in Istanbul

CONTENTS

Introduction

Imagine standing on the edge of a high cliff. You look down and see a huge, colorful land. Your heart beats fast, your hands feel wet, and you want to step back. But you take a deep breath, lean forward, and jump. The wind rushes past you, everything blurs, and for a few exciting seconds, you feel like you are flying. This is BASE jumping. It is one of the most daring sports in the world.

OPPOSITE: BASE jumping in southeastern France

BASE stands for "buildings, antennas, spans (bridges), and earth (cliffs)." Jumpers leap from these tall structures and use a parachute to land safely. The thrill of falling and jumping from different heights makes BASE jumping unique and intense.

Unlike skydiving from a plane, BASE jumping is closer to the ground, making every second thrilling. It takes precision, bravery, and knowledge of how to jump safely. Jumpers must think about the height of the jump, the speed of the wind, and the best place to land. They must know how to control their bodies in the air and how to use their parachutes.

Jumping off of Malaysia's Kuala Lumpur Tower

The First to Fly

The Chinese were the first ones documented to have used small parachute-like devices during gymnastics shows to help with short falls. Historical documents and **artifacts** indicate that as far back as the 11th century, possibly even earlier, Chinese acrobats used these devices during performances, especially in royal courts. The performances were meant to entertain and impress royalty and nobility with thrilling displays of daring and skill.

OPPOSITE: An early parachute descent

These early "parachutes" were basic compared to today's advanced versions. They were likely made from materials such as silk and bamboo and used mainly to slow the descent of performers doing high-altitude acrobatics or stunts.

Over the centuries, the design and concept of these parachute-like devices gradually improved. By the Yuan dynasty (1271–1368 AD), parachute-like devices were regularly used in palace performances. Their use highlights the creativity of inventors and entertainers and shows a progression in understanding aerodynamics and personal safety.

These ancient innovations were the beginnings of uses of parachutes in civilian and military fields. They demonstrated an early grasp of air resistance principles and the use of such forces for controlled descents. This knowledge was important for the development of modern parachuting and has had significant implications for aerospace safety.

By the 16th century, the idea of using parachutes was emerging in Europe. These devices were mainly intended to help people escape from tall stone buildings, such as castles or towers, during fires. Their designs typically involved large, stiff, wooden frameworks covered with cloth. The devices were tested from structures, though experiments were not always successful and were sometimes fatal.

In the early 17th century, Fausto Veranzio, an inventor from Croatia, created his own "parachute." He tested it by jumping from a tower in Venice, Italy. His successful descent demonstrated the practical application of parachutes for safe landings from high places. Veranzio's innovation laid important groundwork for future developments in parachute technology.

The year 1783 was a landmark year in aviation his-

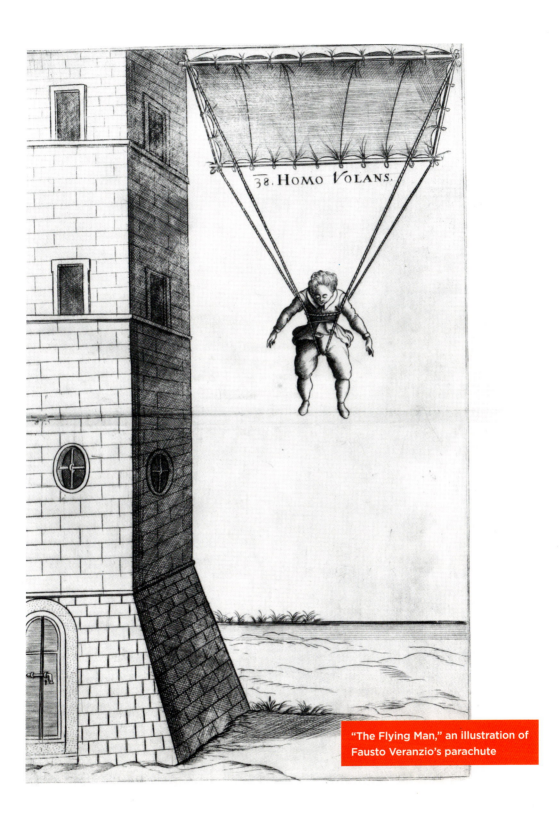

38. HOMO VOLANS.

"The Flying Man," an illustration of Fausto Veranzio's parachute

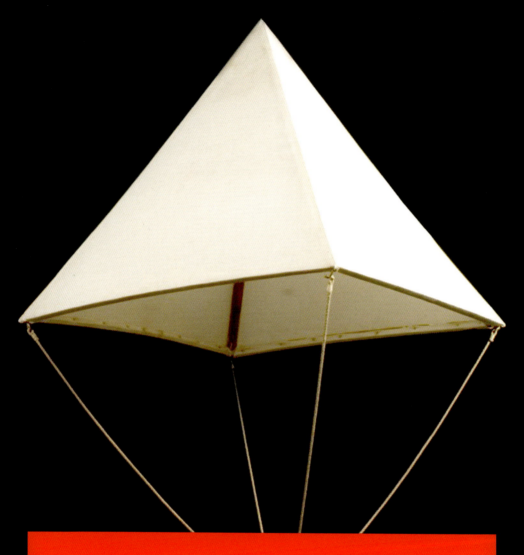

Inspired by Leonardo

Fausto Veranzio, a Renaissance scholar from Croatia, made a significant contribution to the development of parachutes. He was inspired by drawings and writings of earlier inventors, notably Leonardo da Vinci's sketches. Veranzio's design is shown in his book *Machinae Novae* published in 1615. It features a **conical** parachute. Veranzio constructed a **prototype** from a wooden frame and fabric and tested it himself. In 1617, he reportedly jumped from the bell tower of St. Mark's Basilica in Venice, Italy. Veranzio's experiment showed the practical application of parachute technology long before it became widely recognized and used.

tory. It was the year French brothers Joseph-Michel and Jacques-Étienne Montgolfier invented the hot air balloon, opening the door to aerial exploration and travel. In the same year, the Montgolfier brothers also experimented with parachute designs, contributing to the understanding and development of these devices.

Also in 1783, the French scientist Louis-Sébastien Lenormand conducted a successful parachute jump. He jumped from a tall tower with a parachute that had a 14-foot (4.2-meter) diameter. This event is marked as pivotal in the history of parachutes, showing the potential for controlled descent from high places. Lenormand laid important groundwork for the future development of both parachuting and BASE jumping.

Not many people attempted jumps again until 1912. It was at that time that Frederick Rodman Law dared to leap from landmarks such as the Statue of Liberty, the Brooklyn Bridge, and a tall bank building on Wall Street in New York City. His exhibitions captured public interest and showed the potential of parachutes for entertainment and practical purposes.

In the 1940s, an inventive mechanic in Milwaukee, Wisconsin, reportedly made a notable parachute jump from the rafters inside a large blimp hangar. This jump, although not widely publicized, demonstrated the ongoing innovation in parachute use beyond military applications.

In the late 1950s, the adventurous spirit of parachuting continued with Erich Felbermayr, an Austrian dentist. Alongside his colleague Walter Laindecker, Felbermayr executed daring jumps from notable high points in the Dolomites, a mountain range in Italy. The pair chose jump points such as Kleine Zinne, Europabrücke, and Matterhorn. These jumps were among the early instances of what would later be recognized as BASE jumping.

The mid-1960s also saw significant activity in the parachuting community. Mike Pelkey contributed to the sport by parachuting from fixed objects. His highest and most remarkable jump, with the help of Brian Schubert, was on July 24, 1966. The men climbed to the summit of their jump on El Capitan, a vertical rock in Yosemite

The Montgolfier Brothers

In 1783, French brothers Joseph-Michel and Jacques-Étienne Montgolfier made a significant leap in aviation history by inventing the hot air balloon. This invention marked the first successful human flight, paving the way for future aerial exploration. Their initial flight on June 4, 1783, carried a sheep, a duck, and a rooster to test the effects of flight on living creatures. This event started a wave of fascination with flight and led to further innovations in both ballooning and parachuting, including early parachute designs aimed at ensuring safe descents from hot air balloons.

National Park in California. El Capitan is renowned for its staggering height of 7,573 feet (2,308 meters). It provided a dramatic and challenging setting for jumping. Pelkey would participate in and promote BASE jumping for the rest of his life. He even made a memorable jump when he was in his 60s, at the 26th Annual Bridge Day event in 2005.

By the mid-1970s, the practice of jumping from extreme heights was gaining popularity, with notable jumps occurring from the Royal Gorge Bridge in Colorado and the World Trade Center towers in New York City. These events were highly publicized and helped to increase interest in what would soon become known as BASE jumping.

Blazing a Sky Trail

The formal recognition of BASE jumping as a distinct sport came in 1978, largely due to the efforts of Carl Boenish, the "father" of BASE jumping. He was the person who established the acronym BASE, outlining the types of fixed objects from which the first jumps were made. His work led to the formation of the first BASE jumping group, First BASE, which helped to organize the sport.

OPPOSITE: A BASE jump from a mountain cliff in southeastern France

Carl Boenish after a successful jump

Boenish was also a pioneer in using film and photography to advance BASE jumping. He meticulously documented his own jumps and those of others, using the footage and images to review techniques, identify problems, and educate newcomers. Boenish's films, such as the 1984 documentary *Sunshine Superman,* offer a detailed look at his pioneering experiences and the early days of the sport.

Boenish was instrumental in building a community of BASE jumpers. He shared his knowledge widely through seminars and articles, educating others on the right approaches to the sport. He worked to make BASE jumping safer by thorough preparation and deep understanding of the jumping environment. He also stressed the importance of following laws and regulations at potential jump sites, fostering a culture of responsibility in the BASE jumping community.

In addition to his contributions to training and safety, Boenish and his peers made significant adaptations to skydiving equipment for BASE jumping. They modified parachutes to better suit the unique requirements of BASE jumping: shorter fall distances and quick **deployment**.

Skydiving and BASE jumping were more than hobbies for Boenish. They were a significant part of his personal life as well. He even met his wife, Jean Boenish, through skydiving. Jean shared his passion for the sports and often worked with him on various projects and jumps.

Sadly, Boenish's life ended in 1984, during a BASE jumping trip to Norway. Despite his early death, Boenish's influence on skydiving and BASE jumping continues to this day. His commitment to safety and education has left a lasting impact on the sports he loved.

Those who followed in Boenish's footsteps include Chris "Douggs" McDougall, Miles Daisher, Roberta

A jumper in horizontal "flight"

Mancino, and Jeb Corliss. These BASE jumpers pushed the sport's boundaries further, emphasizing innovation and safety.

Jeb Corliss is famous for daring feats such as wingsuit and **proximity flights**. Corliss's parents were international art dealers, so his childhood was filled with travel. It nurtured his adventurous spirit. His early exposure to diverse environments also fueled his fascination with flight and risk-taking.

Corliss has made many notable jumps. He jumped from the Eiffel Tower in Paris, France; the Golden Gate Bridge in San Francisco, California; and the Petronas Towers in Kuala Lumpur, Malaysia. One of his most daring achievements was "flying" through a narrow crack in Tianmen Mountain, China, which he described as one of the most challenging and terrifying experiences of his life. This jump was so significant that it brought him to tears. He was overwhelmed by the intensity and danger of the maneuver.

Corliss's passion for pushing the limits of human flight has not only made him a legend in the BASE jumping community but also a respected figure in media, contributing to the visibility and popularity of the sport. Despite the risks, Corliss is deeply committed to his craft, continually exploring the boundaries of what is possible in human flight.

Jeb Corliss as he flies through Tianmen Mountain, China

Australian Chris "Douggs" McDougall is another well-known figure in the world of extreme sports. His career in skydiving, BASE jumping, and wingsuit flying spans more than 25 years. Douggs has completed more than 4,300 BASE jumps in 42 countries and more than 7,200 skydives! His impressive skills have won him several world records and many championships worldwide.

Douggs is the founder of the Learn to BASE Jump school. His lessons emphasize the importance of safety, thorough training, and understanding the risks involved in skydiving and BASE jumping.

Aside from his athletic pursuits, Douggs is an active public speaker. He calls for pushing beyond personal limits and embracing challenges, not just in sports but in everyday life. Through his talks, he shares lessons learned from his experiences to motivate others to enjoy the

Engineering a Jumper

Carl Boenish studied engineering at Harvey Mudd College in California. He began his career as an electrical engineer at Hughes Aircraft. Boenish moved on to the California Institute of Technology's Jet Propulsion Laboratory, where he worked on important projects—such as the Surveyor moon lander program which helped the National Aeronautics and Space Administration (NASA) prepare for the Apollo missions to the Moon. Boenish's engineering background helped him develop strong understanding and skills as a skydiver, BASE jumper, and filmmaker.

process of overcoming difficulties and achieve their best.

Miles Daisher, another prominent figure in extreme sports, is especially known for his achievements in BASE jumping and skydiving. He has completed more than 7,200 skydives and a whopping 5,500 BASE jumps! He holds the world record for completing the most BASE jumps in one day—63 jumps!

Daisher was born in a military family, which sparked his interest in parachuting. Since 1995, he has been a professional parachutist, constantly seeking to innovate and expand the sport. He is a member of the Red Bull Air Force, an elite team of skydivers, BASE jumpers,

BASE JUMPING

and wingsuit flyers. He has even invented new sports—skayaking and rope swinging. Living in Twin Falls, Idaho, Daisher coaches at Miles D's BASE Camp, where he teaches BASE jumping techniques and safety.

Daisher is not only recognized for his skill in the sports but also for his roles as a Hollywood stunt coordinator and aerial camera specialist. His expertise has led him to work on several film projects. His extensive experience and charm have made him a sought-after figure in media and entertainment. He contributes to various commercials and television shows.

Italian Roberta Mancino is one of the most prominent women to influence BASE jumping. Mancino is a skydiver, BASE jumper, wingsuit flyer, and international model. She began her career in modeling at the age of 16 and took up skydiving when she was 21. Her pursuits

Some BASE jumpers like to push the limit.

in extreme sports have allowed her to perform stunts in stunning locations across the world. Mancino has completed more than 10,000 skydives, and she often blends her adventurous activities with her modeling.

Mancino has won many honors. She holds three world records and two European records in **formation freefly** and has claimed several victories in national and international competitions. The unique combination of modeling and extreme sports has earned her features in major publications. Mancino is a passionate advocate for wingsuit flying as a competitive sport. Her efforts continue to advance it, increasing its development and popularity.

What a Jumper Needs

BASE jumpers have their own language which helps define their practices and culture. Some of this language is shared with skydivers. A "whuffo" is a term jumpers and skydivers use to describe a person who has not yet made a jump. This word comes from "what for?"—as in "what for do you jump from a perfectly good airplane?" "Packing" is the process of folding a parachute in preparation for a jump, a meticulous task crucial for its proper function.

The "exit point" is the specific spot from which a jumper leaps. "Burble" describes the air **turbulence** that can negatively impact parachute deployment. During the jump, the **free fall** is the short period before the parachute is deployed, when jumpers experience pure gravity-driven descent.

BASE jumpers rely on several key pieces of equipment to ensure their jumps are as safe as possible. The most critical component is the parachute. To jump without a parachute would be like trying to skateboard without a deck! The difference in BASE jumping is that the parachute is there to keep you alive—quite literally. So, properly packing the parachute is critical for a safe landing. Additionally, the parachute's canopy is where the "action" happens and where descent control is managed. A container holds the setup securely to the jumper. Ropes, straps, and tethers are used to secure equipment and sometimes aid in the initial descent from fixed objects.

The pilot chute is a small but vital piece of equipment in BASE jumping. It is a small parachute that a jumper manually opens immediately after jumping. The pilot chute catches the air and pulls out the main parachute from its container. This quick deployment is essential for the lower altitudes and shorter freefall times typical of BASE jumps. Without the pilot chute, the main parachute would not open as quickly or smoothly, increasing the risk during the jump.

Helpful Helmets

Helmets help prevent head injuries during BASE jumps. Modern helmets are designed to be lightweight yet incredibly strong, using advanced materials such as carbon fiber and Kevlar. Many helmets also come with built-in communication systems, allowing jumpers to stay in contact with their support team during jumps. Some helmets even have integrated action cameras, enabling jumpers to record their jumps for analysis and sharing. These features not only enhance safety but also contribute to the overall experience, making each jump more enjoyable.

Safety gear includes a helmet to protect against head injuries; a jump suit to streamline and protect the body during freefall; goggles to shield the eyes from high-speed winds; and durable footwear to withstand the impact of landing. Gloves are often used to protect the hands when handling equipment, and communication gear is crucial for coordinating with support teams, especially during complex or filmed jumps.

Another extremely popular and significant advancement—the wingsuit—allows humans to glide through the air with body-fitted, wing-like fabric. The design resembles the body and "wings" of a flying squirrel. It features fabric stretched between the arms, torso, and legs, creating wings that increase surface area and provide lift. The wingsuit extends jumpers' flight times by altering their motion from vertical to horizontal. This innovative suit enables precision and control during flight.

The wingsuit's roots can be traced back to ancient Chinese and Greek mythology. Yet it was not until the late 20th century that a working wingsuit was built, thanks to the pioneering efforts of people such as Patrick de Gayardon, a French skydiver. Gayardon pushed the boundaries of skydiving with design innovations aimed at achieving sustained horizontal flight. In the late 1980s and early 1990s, he experimented with inflatable wing panels. They allowed wearers to adjust lift and maneuverability.

Gayardon's death in 1997 during a skydiving accident was a significant loss to the community, but it did not halt the progress he had inspired. Following in his footsteps, Jari Kuosma, a Finnish parachutist and engineer, refined the wingsuit's design. He focused on aerodynamics and stability. This period saw substantial advancements in materials and technology, making wingsuit flying more accessible and popular among thrill seekers globally.

BASE jumping equipment reflects a deep understanding of aerodynamics, material science, and the nuances of free fall. Several companies have led this technological push. Apex BASE, for example, has introduced its Lobo canopy, which is designed for quick deployment and excellent maneuverability. Similarly, designs from AdrenalinBase—such as the Troll and Ventus canopies—have improved how jumpers handle flight, offering better glide and stability when descending from urban structures or cliffs.

Innovations in parachute design include square and rectangular canopies from Morpheus Technologies and vented canopies—such as the Onyx—from Atair

Fly Like a Squirrel

Wingsuit flying has evolved into both a competitive sport and a form of extreme recreation, in which athletes achieve incredible speeds and perform breathtaking maneuvers. Wingsuit fliers can achieve—depending on various factors such as the design of the wingsuit, the skydiver's body position, and the starting altitude—on average, horizontal speeds between 100 to 200 miles per hour (160 to 320 kilometers per hour)! In 2012, Japanese wingsuit pilot Shin Ito set the world record for the fastest horizontal speed in a wingsuit, topping out at an incredible 202.6 miles per hour (326 km/h)!

Canopies. They handle high speeds and ensure smooth transitions from free fall to controlled flight.

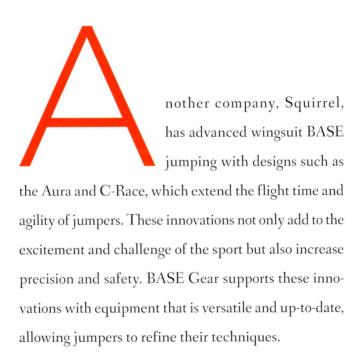

Another company, Squirrel, has advanced wingsuit BASE jumping with designs such as the Aura and C-Race, which extend the flight time and agility of jumpers. These innovations not only add to the excitement and challenge of the sport but also increase precision and safety. BASE Gear supports these innovations with equipment that is versatile and up-to-date, allowing jumpers to refine their techniques.

Not for the Faint-Hearted

BASE jumping gives an excitement like no other sport. Imagine jumping off a tall bridge. For a few seconds, you are falling fast. Your heart races, and everything around you blurs. Then you pull your parachute, and it opens. You float down to the ground, feeling amazing. This is the thrill BASE jumpers love.

OPPOSITE: A BASE jumper leaps off the top of the 400-foot (122-meter) vertical face of the Tombstone in Kane Springs Canyon, Utah.

49

Sky diving is a natural start for many BASE jumpers.

When you fall through the air, the wind rushes past you, and the world moves quickly. Your senses become sharper. You feel every movement and see everything in detail. This exciting feeling is why jumpers keep coming back for more.

Fear is a natural part of BASE jumping. Jumpers use many techniques to manage and overcome it. Gradual exposure to heights helps. The jumpers start with small jumps and work their way up to higher ones to build confidence. Focusing on skills also helps. Jumpers practice packing parachutes, checking gear, and planning jumps. Knowing they are well-prepared helps them manage fear and focus on the jump.

Many jumpers start with skydiving to build their skills. Skydiving helps them get used to freefall and parachute control. After many skydives, they are ready to try BASE jumping.

Mindfulness helps jumpers to stay calm and focused. Mindfulness is about being present and aware. Techniques such as deep breathing and visualization improve mental clarity and reduce anxiety. Jumpers practice deep breathing to stay calm. Visualization involves mentally rehearsing the jump, from the moment of the leap to the safe landing.

Some jumpers also practice meditation to improve their focus. Meditation helps clear the mind and reduce stress. A clear, focused mind is crucial for making quick, accurate decisions during the jump.

BASE jumping is exciting, but also very risky. There are more accidents and injuries in it than in many other sports. Jumpers need to know about the dangers—equipment failures, sudden weather changes, and not landing correctly. Jumpers must be very careful and ready to handle these risks by preparing well, continually training, and always following safety rules.

Safety measures in BASE jumping cover many things. Jumpers need to know how to pack their parachutes correctly, how to take care of their equipment, and what to do if something goes wrong. They also need to understand the challenges of each jump site—the wind conditions, the terrain, and any obstacles they might face.

New technology has made BASE jumping safer. Modern parachutes, tracking devices, and weather prediction tools help jumpers make good decisions and reduce risks. Tracking devices can show where a jumper is, which helps in case of an emergency. Weather prediction tools help jumpers understand the weather and choose the best time to jump.

Even with all the risks, BASE jumping offers amazing rewards. The feeling of freedom, the rush of adrenaline,

The Steps in a Jump

Before a jump, the jumpers secure permits and ensure compliance with environmental regulations. They must scout and prepare the landing site, ensuring it is safe and clear of obstacles. A support team, possibly including a film crew, coordinates the **logistics** and safety steps. On jump day, the jumpers travel to the exit point, sometimes involving a hike or climb in remote areas. They check every strap, buckle, and stitch on their gear. Upon exiting, they experience a few seconds of free fall before deploying the parachute. They guide their descent with advanced body techniques and use practiced maneuvers to land precisely at the chosen spot.

and the success of completing a challenging jump make it all worthwhile to the jumpers. BASE jumping lets you see the world from a new perspective and gives you a strong sense of achievement.

When jumpers are in the air, they feel like they are flying. They see the world from high up and feel a great sense of freedom. Landing safely after a jump gives them a huge sense of accomplishment. This feeling is why many jumpers love the sport so much.

The rewards of BASE jumping are not just physical. Many jumpers say that the sport helps them grow as people. It challenges them to face their fears, push their limits, and become more confident. They learn to stay calm under pressure, make quick decisions, and trust their training and equipment. This growth makes them stronger and more resilient in other parts of their lives.

The BASE jumping community is very important. Jumpers support each other, share tips and advice, and help each other stay safe. They often form close friendships that last a lifetime. Jumpers travel together to different jump sites and share their experiences. They celebrate each other's successes and help each other through challenges. Being part of this community makes BASE jumping even more special.

Mentors play a big role in the BASE jumping community. They help new jumpers learn the skills they need and give them confidence. Mentors teach jumpers how to pack parachutes, check gear, and plan jumps. Having a mentor makes a big difference for new jumpers. They feel more confident and prepared with someone experienced to guide them. Mentors also help jumpers understand the importance of safety and preparation.

The world of BASE jumping competitions is not well known. It occurs away from the spotlight of events such as the X Games or the Olympics. Nevertheless, BASE jumping has grown into a structured sport with its own set of standards and contests. Participants looking to enter these competitions are required to have a certain level of experience, usually a minimum number of previous jumps. It helps ensure the safety of all competitors.

The contests feature various categories, each with its own rules. For instance, wingsuit BASE jumping and tracking are popular categories that attract participants who specialize in these styles. Competitions such as the BASE Jump Extreme World Championship and the World BASE Race highlight these categories, drawing skilled jumpers from around the globe. The World BASE Race, in particular, focuses on wingsuit BASE jump-

Blowing in the Wind

Wind conditions play a crucial role in the safety and success of a BASE jump. Jumpers must carefully evaluate wind speed and direction before leaping. Strong winds can push a jumper off course, potentially leading to collisions with the object they jumped from or nearby structures. Light winds or calm conditions are ideal, as they allow for more precise control during free fall and parachute deployment. Experienced jumpers often use wind meters to measure wind conditions at the jump site and at the landing area, to ensure a safe and controlled descent.

ing and is known for being inclusive, encouraging fun jumpers to participate alongside seasoned competitors.

One of the more significant organizations on the competitive scene is the World Wingsuit League, which was established in 2012. It has gained substantial popularity, especially in China, where some events have attracted more than 390 million viewers! Similarly, the BASE Jump Extreme World Championship annually selects 20 elite jumpers from a global pool to compete across various disciplines. Competitors in this championship are required to have completed at least 150 BASE jumps, including 10 jumps within the three months leading up to the competition. It makes sure that all participants are actively engaged and highly skilled.

Competitions in BASE jumping are not only about performance—such as accuracy in landing—but also incorporate artistic elements—such as acrobatics during free fall. These artistic competitions add a creative dimension to the sport, challenging jumpers to blend physical skill with expressive movement.

Overall, competitive BASE jumping is becoming increasingly popular and accessible, continually pushing the boundaries of what is possible within the sport. It provides an exciting platform for jumpers to exchange knowledge, learn from one another, and have fun, all while advancing their skills and contributing to the sport's evolution.

If being left out of the Olympics or major events like the X Games lessens the sport's visibility compared to well-funded, mainstream sports, that's acceptable to many jumpers. To them, BASE jumping is about a personal challenge against fear and gravity, rather than formal recognition.

BASE jumpers "fly" after jumping from the Ostankino TV tower in Moscow, Russia.

Jumping into the Future

Advances in materials science and technology are driving improvements in BASE jumping equipment. Parachutes are made from lighter, stronger materials that provide better control and stability during descent. These materials include advanced fabrics such as ripstop nylon and Kevlar that resist wear and tear. Additionally, **GPS** and **AI**-assisted navigation systems are being integrated into gear to offer jumpers real-time information on wind patterns and ideal deployment times.

OPPOSITE: A man doing a BASE jump with a parachute from a cable car in France

These technologies enhance both the safety and accuracy of jumps, allowing for more precise landings and reducing the risk of accidents.

Technologies such as augmented reality (AR) may soon allow jumpers to simulate jumps in various conditions and environments without making an actual leap. It would greatly enhance skills and preparation, particularly for jumps in new and challenging locations. Meanwhile, wingsuit designs are expected to dramatically evolve, with new models promising longer, more controlled flights. Engineers believe these suits may soon enable extended flights, thanks to compact propulsion systems that could allow for nearly endless flight durations.

BASE jumping is growing to new and more extreme places. Jumpers are exploring more urban areas with tall buildings and remote cliffs—and even the idea of jumping from space! Advances in space travel and technology are making it possible to think about jumping from the edge of space.

n 2012, Austrian skydiver Felix Baumgartner did the famous Red Bull Stratos jump. While he didn't jump from space itself, he did jump from the stratosphere—a layer high up in the Earth's atmosphere. Baumgartner ascended to a staggering altitude of 128,100 feet (39,045 m) in a helium-filled balloon, before jumping and free-falling for several minutes. During his descent, he became the first human to break the sound barrier—

Felix Baumgartner jumps out of a capsule during the famous Red Bull Stratos jump in 2012.

travel faster than the speed of sound—without a vehicle!

Baumgartner's jump showed what is possible with high-altitude jumps. It was very dangerous and needed a lot of preparation and special equipment. The jumper wore a special suit to protect him from the cold and thin air. The jump inspired many people and showed the amazing possibilities of BASE jumping.

BASE jumping and skydiving have not only challenged human limits but have also significantly influenced popular culture. Movies such as *Point Break*—both the 1991 original and the 2015 remake—have introduced audiences worldwide to the thrill of skydiving and BASE jumping, showing these activities as part of stories about friendship, adventure, and the pursuit of extremes. The scenes of Patrick Swayze and Keanu Reeves in the original, and the breathtaking wingsuit flight sequences in the remake, show the sports in a way that blends action with a sense of freedom, leaving a lasting impression on viewers.

Similarly, *Transformers: Dark of the Moon* features wingsuit flyers gliding through Chicago's skyscrapers, mixing Hollywood fantasy with the real-life capabilities of human flight. This movie shows the skill and fearlessness of BASE jumpers. *The Expendables* 3 offers a glimpse into the precision and teamwork required in skydiving, as the team executes a high-stakes aerial feat, highlighting the sport's potential for both entertainment and military application.

Media exposure has been a factor in the growth and development of BASE jumping. High-definition cameras and drones now offer viewers a close-up and personal look at the action, bringing the experience of free fall and canopy flight into homes around the world. This visibility has highlighted the skills and daring of legendary jumpers and attracted new enthusiasts to the sport.

Social media platforms such as Instagram, YouTube, and TikTok increase the visibility and popularity of BASE jumping. High-quality videos showing jumps from cliffs, bridges, and buildings attract millions of views, helping jumpers gain recognition and followers. This visibility

A BASE jumper descends off the Tombstone in Kane Springs Canyon, Utah.

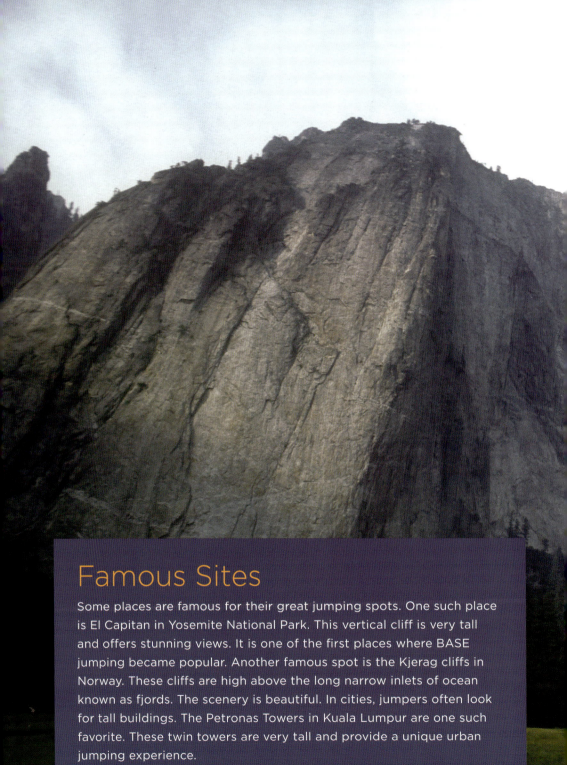

Famous Sites

Some places are famous for their great jumping spots. One such place is El Capitan in Yosemite National Park. This vertical cliff is very tall and offers stunning views. It is one of the first places where BASE jumping became popular. Another famous spot is the Kjerag cliffs in Norway. These cliffs are high above the long narrow inlets of ocean known as fjords. The scenery is beautiful. In cities, jumpers often look for tall buildings. The Petronas Towers in Kuala Lumpur are one such favorite. These twin towers are very tall and provide a unique urban jumping experience.

can lead to sponsorships and collaborations, as brands are keen to associate with the high-adrenaline, visually striking content that BASE jumpers produce.

Social media also fosters a global community of BASE jumpers. These platforms allow jumpers to share their experiences, tips, and safety practices. They provide a space for newcomers to learn from experienced jumpers.

Social media exposure can have both positive and negative psychological effects. On the one hand, sharing experiences and receiving recognition from followers can be rewarding and affirming for jumpers. On the other hand, the desire to create increasingly daring content to maintain social media engagement can push jumpers to take greater risks and make them much less safe.

As BASE jumping grows, it is important to think about the laws and ethics of the sport. Jumpers need to know and follow the rules and laws of the places they jump. It helps keep the sport safe and respected. Respecting nature and the environment is also crucial. Jumpers should leave no trace and be mindful of their impact on the areas they visit. Promoting safety and responsible practices is key to the future of BASE jumping. It helps protect jump sites and ensures that the sport can continue to grow.

BASE jumping will continue to be a thrilling and fast-changing sport. The improvements in equipment, the exploration of new jump sites, and the growth of the community all point to a bright future. BASE jumping teaches important lessons about preparation, trust, and overcoming fear. It brings people together and pushes them to achieve amazing things.

Each jump is a ballet in the sky, a flight of the human spirit across the vast canvas of the Earth, a testament to the dreams that propel us ever onward. In the free fall, in the rush of the wind and the roar of the quiet above the clouds, jumpers find a freedom that is both exhilarating and peaceful—a reminder of what it means to be truly alive in a world boundless with possibilities.

Astronautical Heights

High-altitude jumps, such as the famous Red Bull Stratos jump by Felix Baumgartner, require specialized technology to ensure safety and success. Jumpers must wear **pressurized suits** to protect against the extreme cold and low oxygen levels found at high altitudes. These suits are similar to suits used by astronauts, providing necessary insulation and oxygen supply. Additionally, high-altitude balloons or aircraft are needed to reach the jump altitude. Advanced navigation systems and tracking devices monitor the jumper's position and ensure a safe descent. These technologies have made it possible to push the limits of human flight and explore new frontiers in BASE jumping.

Selected Bibliography

"BASE Jumping: How It Began." Bridge Day, October 16, 2009. https://officialbridgeday.com/bridge-blog/basejumping-how-it-began.

Carter, Kenneth. *BUZZ!: Inside the Minds of Thrill-Seekers, Daredevils, and Adrenaline Junkies.* Cambridge University Press, 2019.

Greenspan, Judy. *Daring and Dangerous: Sky Jumpers.* Rourke Educational Media, 2019.

Patterson, Thom. "Meet the Father of BASE Jumping." CNN, January 15, 2016. https://www.cnn.com/2016/01/14/us/sunshine-superman-carl-boenish-base-jumping/index.html.

Renhard, James. "Base Jumping: Everything You Need to Know." Mpora, February 12, 2016.

https://mpora.com/skydiving-wingsuits/base-jumping-everything-need-know/.

"What Is BASE Jumping? The Thrilling Sport of Speed, Adrenaline, and Danger." 2022. Crawl Bars, September 9, 2022. https://www.trycrawl.com/common-questions/what-is-base-jumping-the-thrilling-sport-of-speed-adrenaline-and-danger.

Glossary

adrenaline	a hormone that helps a person react quickly in a dangerous, stressful, or exiting situation
aerodynamics	the study of the properties of moving air and how it interacts with solid objects
AI	short for "artificial intelligence"; technology that allows computers to perform tasks traditionally performed by humans
artifact	an object made by humans, especially a tool used in the past
augmented reality	technology that overlays digital information, such as images, sounds, or other data, onto the real-world environment
conical	shaped like a cone, pointy
deployment	in parachuting, the initial opening of a parachute
formation freefly	a discipline in which a group of jumpers perform synchronized free-fall maneuvers and formations at varying orientations, including head-up, head-down, and flat-flying positions
free fall	the part of a jump when a jumper is falling under the force of gravity before deploying the parachute
GPS	short for "global positioning system"; technology used to get real-time information on location and environmental conditions

logistics	the process of obtaining, moving, organizing, and managing resources for something
pressurized suit	a suit that provides insulation and oxygen, used for high-altitude jumps to protect jumpers from extreme cold and low oxygen levels
propulsion	the force by which something is pushed along
prototype	a model
proximity flight	a type of wingsuit flight in which the jumper flies very close to the ground, cliffs, or other obstacles to achieve a sense of speed and danger
rope swinging	an activity where a jumper swings from a long rope attached to a high structure, such as a bridge or cliff, and then releases to enter free fall
simulate	to pretend
skayaking	an extreme sport that combines kayaking and skydiving; the jumper uses a specially designed kayak to perform aerial maneuvers after jumping from an aircraft or a high object
skydiving	the sport of jumping from an aircraft and performing acrobatic maneuvers before deploying a parachute to land
tracking	a technique in skydiving and BASE jumping which involves a jumper moving horizontally through the air to cover more distance during free fall, created by adjusting the body position to create more lift and forward motion
turbulence	unstable movement of air caused by changes in wind speed and direction

Websites

Academic Kids: Base Jumping
https://academickids.com/encyclopedia/index.php/BASE_
   jumping
Learn about BASE jumping history, equipment and techniques,
   and legal issues.

PBS Learning Media
https://www.pbslearningmedia.org/
Search for videos, interactive activities, and other materials
   related to extreme sports.

Snake River BASE Academy
https://www.snakeriverbase.com/
Read detailed information about BASE jumping from the staff
   of a well-known BASE jumping school.

Index